D0017205

A Girl Named
Helen

The True Story of
HELEN KELLER

By **Bonnie Bader**

Illustrated by **Melissa Manwill**

Scholastic Inc.

Published by Scholastic Inc., *Publishers since 1920.* SCHOLASTIC and associated logos are trademarks and/or registered trademarks of Scholastic Inc. The publisher does not have any control over and does not assume any responsibility for author or third-party websites or their content.

No part of this publication may be reproduced, stored in a retrieval system, or transmitted in any form or by any means, electronic, mechanical, photocopying, recording, or otherwise, without written permission of the publisher. For information regarding permission, write to Scholastic Inc., Attention: Permissions Department, 557 Broadway, New York, NY 10012.

Photos ©: 44: Rolls Press/Popperfoto/Getty Images; 45: Courtesy of Perkins School for the Blind Archives, Watertown, MA; 46: Associated Press/AP Images; 47: Rick Madonik/Getty Images.

Illustrated by Melissa Manwill
Book design by Suzanne LaGasa

© 2018 American Girl. All American Girl marks are trademarks of American Girl. Used under license by Scholastic Inc.

Library of Congress Cataloging-in-Publication Data Available

ISBN 978-1-338-19303-9

10 9 8 7 6 5 4 3 2 1   18 19 20 21 22

Printed in the U.S.A.   23
First printing 2018

Contents

Introduction

Helen Keller became **deaf** and **blind** when she was a small child in the 1800s. At that time, not many deaf people learned to communicate. But Helen did. Not many blind people learned to read and write. But Helen did. Helen wrote books, gave speeches, and traveled around the world. Through her determination and courage, Helen Keller became a role model for anyone facing extraordinary challenges.

Chapter 1

Changes

On June 27, 1880, a healthy baby girl was born in Tuscumbia, Alabama. Her parents, Arthur and Kate Keller, named her Helen.

Helen's family loved her very much. She was a fun and beautiful baby. And she was very smart. By six months, Helen could say a few words: *tea* and *wa-wah*, which meant *water*. At the age of one, Helen started to walk.

When Helen was about a year and a half old, she got a very high fever. Helen's doctor was not sure what was wrong with her. He called her sickness "brain fever." For several days, her parents thought she might die. Then her fever went away. Her family was relieved.

Later, Helen's mother passed her hands in front of Helen's face. Helen just stared straight ahead—she couldn't see a thing. When the bell rang for dinner, Helen couldn't hear the sound. Not only was Helen blind, she was deaf, too.

Helen's parents took her to a doctor, but he said there was nothing he could do to help. Helen Keller's world was now dark and silent.

Chapter 2

Learning to Communicate

Most children learn to speak by listening and watching others talk. Helen could not listen. She could not watch. Therefore, she could not speak. But that did not stop little Helen from exploring and noticing the world around her. She followed her mother around wherever she went by holding onto her skirts. She sniffed the air for different smells. She felt vibrations when people moved.

In those days, there were hardly any schools for deaf or blind children in the entire United States. But Helen began to figure out her own ways to communicate.

When she pulled someone, it meant *come*. When she pushed someone, it meant *go*.

Still, Helen couldn't always express herself in a way that was easy for others to understand. When she couldn't communicate her thoughts, she would get angry. Helen would kick and scream, and it was hard for her parents to control her.

When Helen had her temper under control, she loved to explore the garden. She learned to tell the plants apart just by their smell and feel.

Helen also spent time with her dog, Belle. Helen tried teaching Belle her signs, but Belle never caught on. She was more interested in chasing birds in the garden!

When Helen was five, she got a big surprise — a baby sister named Mildred! Helen was jealous of all the attention her sister got. One day she tipped over the cradle while Mildred was in it. Luckily, Mildred was not hurt. However, it was clear that Helen's anger could hurt herself and others. Helen's parents felt sure she would become less frustrated if she learned how to communicate better.

In Washington, DC, the Kellers met with Dr. Alexander Graham Bell. When Helen walked into Dr. Bell's office with her parents, she climbed right up into the doctor's lap!

Dr. Bell suggested that the Kellers write to the Perkins Institution for the Blind in Boston, Massachusetts, and ask if they had a teacher for Helen.

Chapter 3

A Teacher Arrives

On March 3, 1887, six-year-old Helen stood outside on her porch. She felt the vibrations of a horse-drawn carriage coming closer and closer. The carriage stopped and Helen held out her arms, expecting her mother. But instead she touched a stranger! Helen did not like strangers, but she was curious. Who was this new person?

It was Anne Sullivan, a twenty-year-old recent graduate of the Perkins Institution. She would live with the Kellers as Helen's teacher.

The next morning, as Helen helped Anne unpack her bags, Helen found a doll. Anne took Helen's hand and spelled out the letters for the word *doll* on her palm. Helen thought

the doll now belonged to her. When Anne took back the doll, Helen had a temper tantrum. Anne tried to calm her down, but Helen just grew more and more angry.

Helen and her new teacher were not off to a good start.

Helen's temper tantrums continued. One day, Helen tried to eat food from Anne's plate. When Anne stopped her, Helen became furious. She kicked and screamed. She refused to use a spoon to eat her own food.

Everything with Helen was a battle. The Kellers tried to help, but Anne realized the best thing to do was to get Helen away from her family so she could focus. Anne and Helen would live in the cottage that was near the main house.

Although they were alone, things between Helen and Anne did not get better. The two had lots of battles about everyday tasks like getting dressed and eating. But Anne did not give up trying to teach Helen.

One day, Anne took Helen outside to the water pump. Anne put one of Helen's hands under the cold water and took her other hand and spelled out the letters for the word *water*. W-A-T-E-R. Suddenly, Helen understood!

A thrill ran through Helen's body. That day Anne spelled a lot of other words into Helen's hand, including the word *teacher*. For the first time, Helen felt hope. Her dark world was starting to brighten.

Chapter 4

A New World Opens

Once she learned the alphabet, Helen could communicate with her parents. Anne spelled what her parents said into Helen's hand. Helen spelled what she wanted to say back.

Anne also used the world outside as Helen's classroom. They studied nature. Helen learned what happened when a seed was planted in the ground by feeling it grow a tiny bit each day.

By the summer of 1887, Anne gave Helen a few pieces of cardboard with the letters of the alphabet written in raised lettering. Helen touched the words and learned what they said.

Anne also taught Helen how to write with a grooved wooden writing board. A piece of paper was placed over the board. Helen used the grooves to guide her pencil and form letters.

Months after Helen learned the alphabet, she began learning to read using a system for the blind called **Braille**.

Anne was very proud of her student. She wrote letters to the director of the Perkins Institution about Helen's progress. Her letters eventually led to stories about Helen in the Boston newspapers. Helen was becoming famous.

Chapter 5

Special Invitations

In May 1888, seven-year-old Helen received an invitation to visit the White House to meet President Grover Cleveland!

President Cleveland was amazed at what Helen had accomplished. Helen Keller, a deaf and blind young girl, had shown the world how strong and smart she was. And there was more to come.

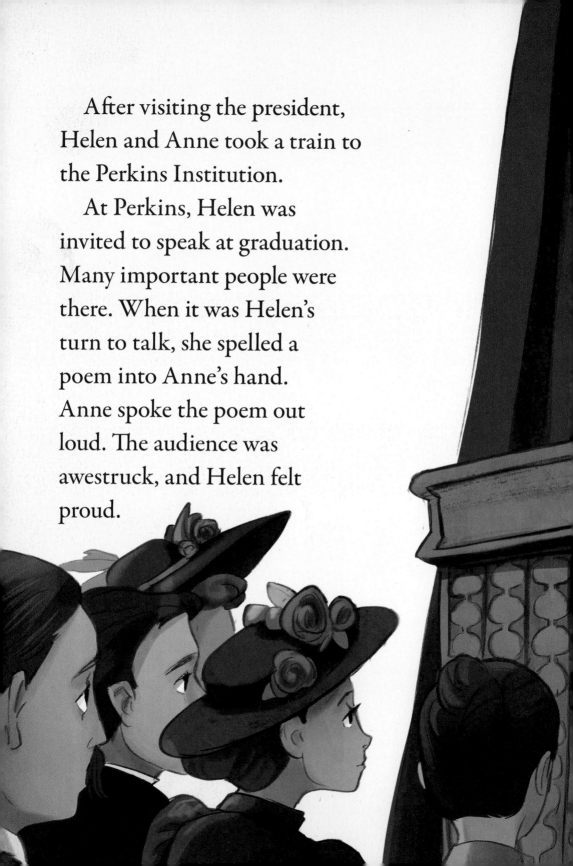

After visiting the president,
Helen and Anne took a train to
the Perkins Institution.

At Perkins, Helen was
invited to speak at graduation.
Many important people were
there. When it was Helen's
turn to talk, she spelled a
poem into Anne's hand.
Anne spoke the poem out
loud. The audience was
awestruck, and Helen felt
proud.

In October, Helen returned to Perkins as a student. Helen studied music, clay modeling, and basket weaving.

Although Helen could read and write, she still could not talk. When Helen was nine, Anne found a teacher in Boston to help. Helen learned how lips moved when someone talked by touching the new teacher's mouth.

She practiced and practiced, but no sound came out. One day, Helen opened her mouth and said, "It is warm." Her words were not clear, and only the speech teacher and Anne could understand her—but she was speaking! Although Helen would never learn to speak clearly, she had accomplished another goal.

Chapter 6

College Dreams

After studying in Boston, fourteen-year-old Helen went to a New York City school for deaf children. Of course, Anne went with her.

Helen's classes included lip reading, speech, math, French, and German. And she went on field trips, too. Helen and her class visited the Statue of Liberty, where she climbed to the top!

Living in New York City expanded Helen's world. Next, she set a new goal for herself: to go to college. At that time, few women went to college. And there had never been a deaf and blind woman to finish college. But that didn't discourage Helen.

In 1896, she enrolled in the Cambridge School for Young Ladies. Unlike her school in New York, this school was for the hearing as well. Helen had to work extra hard to keep up with her studies, and all the studying made her weak and tired. Helen's mother thought Anne

was pushing her too hard, and that maybe it was time to separate the two of them. Anne and Helen were both terribly upset at the idea of being separated from each other. In the end, Anne stayed.

At last, Helen's dream came true: She was accepted to Radcliffe, a **prestigious** women's college.

Radcliffe was hard. Anne went to classes with Helen and spelled into her hand as the teachers spoke.

When she wasn't studying, Helen wrote down stories about her life. An editor from a magazine offered Helen $3,000 to publish them, and she agreed. Eventually, a teacher at Harvard named John Macy offered to put the stories together in a book. Helen's book, *The Story of My Life*, was published in 1903.

Helen graduated from Radcliffe in 1904 with honors for her high grades. Newspapers around the world wrote about Helen Keller: the first blind and deaf person to graduate from an American college.

Chapter 7

A Life of Accomplishment

After college, Helen continued to amaze the world. In 1913, she gave a public speech for the first time. When Helen got on the stage, she panicked. She forgot how to make her words come out properly. At the end of the speech, Helen ran off the stage in tears. She felt like a failure. She didn't think the audience liked her—but they did! She continued to give speeches for the next fifty years.

Helen gave speeches about her life. She explained the challenges blind and deaf people faced. With Anne, Helen traveled all over the United States, and even to Europe and Japan, as an **advocate** for people with **disabilities**. She also marched for women's **suffrage**, or the right to vote.

Helen never let any obstacle stop her. The same determination that made her throw tantrums of frustration when she was a child gave her the strength to pursue education and fight for others.

On June 1, 1968, Helen Keller died. The world will never forget this brave, smart, and determined woman.

GLOSSARY

ADVOCATE: a person who publicly supports a specific cause or policy

AUTISM: a mental condition that causes difficulty in communicating and forming relationships with other people

BLIND: unable to see

BRAILLE: a form of written language that allows the blind to read by feeling raised patterns and dots with their fingertips

DEAF: unable to hear

DISABILITY: the lack of ability, strength, or power to do something

PRESTIGIOUS: respected

SUFFRAGE: the right to vote in a political election

Helen with her teacher, Anne

TIMELINE

1880: Helen is born in Tuscumbia, Alabama

1882: Helen contracts a serious illness that renders her deaf and blind

1886: Helen and her family visit Dr. Alexander Graham Bell

1887: Anne Sullivan moves in with the Keller family to become Helen's teacher

Helen as a young girl, circa 1888

1888: Helen and Anne travel to the Perkins Institution to continue Helen's education

1894: Helen attends school in New York City

1896: Helen attends the Cambridge School for Young Ladies to prepare for college

1900: Helen attends Radcliffe College in Massachusetts

Helen as a graduate of Radcliffe College

1903: Helen's autobiography and her first book, *The Story of My Life*, is published

1904: Helen becomes the first deaf and blind person to earn a college degree when she graduates from Radcliffe College

1919–1924: Helen tours the United States, giving speeches

1924: Helen becomes the spokesperson for the American Foundation for the Blind

1936: Anne Sullivan, Helen's longtime teacher and friend, dies

1946: Helen begins a series of world tours over 11 years, eventually traveling to 35 countries to advocate on behalf of people with disabilities

1964: President Lyndon B. Johnson awards Helen with the Presidential Medal of Freedom

1968: Helen passes away at her home in Connecticut

A GIRL NAMED CARLY

There are a lot of young girls helping to make positive changes in our world today, just like Helen Keller did. Carly Fleischmann is one of those girls.

When Carly Fleischmann was a toddler, her parents noticed that she was not keeping up with her twin sister. When she was two, they found out why: Carly is **autistic** and has oral-motor apraxia, which makes her unable to speak.

As a young child, Carly got a lot of therapy. She learned to walk, but she still could not speak. Frustrated, Carly would often have temper tantrums. Some people suggested that

Carly be sent to a group home. But her parents refused. Her father said that when he looked into her eyes, he could see that she was smart.

Carly really wanted to find her voice, but how? When she was ten, Carly began typing what she wanted to say on a keyboard. It was hard for Carly to type, since she had trouble using her fingers. At first, all she could get out were one-word sentences. But Carly did not give up until she was able to communicate through typing.

Today, Carly has a successful Internet talk show called *Speechless with Carly Fleischmann*. She interviews celebrities like Channing Tatum. She is the very first nonverbal celebrity talk show host!

Carly is also an advocate for people with autism. She wants others to understand that all autistic people aren't the same. Carly said, "I am autistic but that is not who I am. Take time to know me, before you judge me."